RISE & SHINE

STAAR Prep
Grade 2
Reading Comprehension
Second Edition

by Jonathan D. Kantrowitz
Edited by Katherine Pierpont

Item Code RAS 2579 • Copyright © 2017 Queue, Inc.

All rights reserved. No part of the material protected by this copyright may be reproduced or utilized in any form or by any means, electronic or mechanical, including photocopying, recording, or by any information storage and retrieval system. Printed in the United States of America.

Queue, Inc.• P.O. Box 156 • Fairfield, CT 06824
(800) 232-2224 • Fax: (800) 775-2729 • www.qworkbooks.com

Table of Contents

To the Students......v
Dogs Don't Dance......1
All About Goldfish......6
Painting a Room......10
Frogs......14
The Star *by Jane Taylor*......17
The Ant and the Grasshopper *adapted from Aesop's fables*......20
Making Banana Bread......23
Robin......27
The Bear Facts......30
The House Sparrow......33
Iggy......36
The Cow *by Robert Louis Stevenson*......40
The Olympics......43
The Bald Eagle......46
Planting a Flower Garden......49
Summer All Year Long......52
Awesome Adventures......55
Traffic......58
The Rat Princess......62
Jenny Wren Arrives......67
Wetland: More Than Just a Swamp......73
The Golden Fingers......78
Why the Morning Glory Climbs......82
The Pig Brother......86
Why the Evergreen Trees Keep Their Leaves in Winter......91
Saving the Birds......96
Speaking a Piece......102
Raggylug......108

To the Students

In this reading comprehension workbook, you will read many fiction and nonfiction passages, as well as some poetry. You will then answer multiple-choice and open-ended questions about what you have read.

As you read and answer the questions, please remember:

- You may refer back to the text as often as you like.
- Read each question very carefully and choose the **best** answer.
- Indicate the correct multiple-choice answers directly in this workbook. Circle or underline the correct answer.
- Write your open-ended responses directly on the lines provided. If you need more space, use a separate piece of paper to complete your answer.

Tips for Answering Multiple-Choice Questions

Multiple-choice questions have a stem, which is a question or an incomplete sentence, followed by three answer choices. You should select only one answer choice. The following are some tips to help you correctly answer multiple-choice questions on the CRCT Grade 2 Reading Test:

- Read each passage carefully.
- Read each question and think about the answer. You may look back to the reading selection as often as necessary.
- Answer all questions on your answer sheet. Do not mark any answers to questions in your test booklet.
- For each question, choose the best answer, and completely fill in the circle in the space provided on your answer sheet.
- If you do not know the answer to a question, skip it and go on. You may return to it later if you have time.
- If you finish the section of the test that you are working on early, you may review your answers in that section only. Don't go on to the next section of the test.

Here are some guidelines to remember when writing your open-ended answers:

- Organize your ideas and express them clearly.
- Correctly organize and separate your paragraphs.
- Support your ideas with examples when necessary.
- Make your writing interesting and enjoyable to read.
- Check your spelling and use of grammar and punctuation.
- Your answers should be accurate and complete.

DOGS DON'T DANCE

Lucy the dog loved watching the birds. The birds would dance across the grass when no one was looking. They seemed very happy as they hopped around the yard. Lucy wanted to dance with the birds. But they flew away every time she got close.

Lucy sat sadly in the yard. She heard a "tweet! tweet!" from high above. It was a bluebird in the tree.

"What do you want, dog?" asked the bluebird. "Why do you chase us?"

"I don't want to chase you," said Lucy. "I only want to dance with you."

The bluebird laughed loudly. "Dogs don't dance," said the bird. "You are too large. You will fall."

Lucy knew she could dance if she tried. She was a clever little dog.

"Show me," said Lucy. "I will learn the steps."

The bird jumped around the yard as Lucy watched carefully. When he finished, Lucy danced. The bird was pleased. This dog could dance!

The other birds came to watch the little dog. The animals happily danced together every day. Lucy proved that dogs could do anything!

1. This story is make-believe because the

   A. animals talk to each other.
   B. birds hop around the yard.
   C. dog chases the birds away.

   This question asks you to think about what makes this story make-believe. You can tell when a story is make-believe when something happens in the story that couldn't happen in real life. Look at the answer choices. The first one says that the animals talk to each other. Answer choice A is good choice because you know that animals can't really talk to each other. Look at answer choice B. Birds hop around yards in real life, so this isn't right. Dogs can also chase birds in real life, so answer choice C is not right. The best answer is A.

2. This story is mostly about a

   A. happy bluebird.
   B. dog who wants to dance.
   C. dog who needs a friend.

   This question asks you what the story is mostly about. The bluebird is in the story, but he is not the main character. You can cross off answer choice A. This story is about a dog who wants to dance, so answer choice A is not a good choice. Lucy is friendly, but she is not looking for a friend in the story. Answer choice C is not right. Answer choice B is best.

It was a bluebird in the tree.

3. Which word has two word parts?

   A. was
   B. tree
   C. bluebird

   This question asks you to find the word that has more than one syllable. A syllable is a part of a word. Look at answer choice A. The word was has only one part. This is not the right answer. Tree also has one word part. So answer choice B is wrong. Bluebird has two word parts. This means answer choice C is the best answer.

4. Another good title for this story would be

   A. "The Mean Bluebird."
   B. "A Dancing Dog."
   C. "Chasing Birds Away."

   Think about the story you have just read. A title tells you a little about the story. Answer choice A isn't a good choice. The bluebird was not really mean. Answer choice B is good because the story is about a dancing dog. Answer choice C is not right. Lucy does not mean to chase the birds away. Answer choice B is the best answer.

5. In this story, the word <u>proved</u> means
   A. showed.
   B. played.
   C. dreamed.

   This question asks you to figure out the meaning of a word. Look at the sentence where this word is found: *Lucy proved that dogs could do anything!* You can try putting each of the answer choices into the sentence to try to find the answer. *Showed* fits well in the sentence, so answer choice A may be correct. *Played* does not fit, so answer choice B is not right. *Dreamed* does not fit either. Answer choice C is incorrect. Answer choice A is best.

6. What lesson does this story teach? Use information from the story in your answer.

   For this question, you will have to write a few sentences about what lesson this story teaches. Think about what was important in the story. What do you think the author wanted the readers to learn? Use these ideas in your answer.

   Sample response:

   I think that the lesson of this story is that you can do anything. Even though Lucy was a dog, she wanted to do dance. She believed that she could do it. By carefully watching the bird, she could see how he danced. Once she put her mind to it, Lucy found herself dancing.

ALL ABOUT GOLDFISH

You might know someone who has a goldfish. These fish make very good pets. The goldfish you see in homes are small. But some goldfish can grow very large. The biggest goldfish known weighed nine pounds! Most goldfish are orange but some are black, brown, or gray. Some fish have many different colors on their bodies.

Wild goldfish can live for almost 50 years. Many goldfish live in small ponds. Fish that are kept in homes live for many years as well. Goldfish enjoy being around other fish. You may want to keep two goldfish together. This way the fish will not be <u>lonely</u>.

Goldfish are very easy to care for. You can buy their food at a pet store, and it doesn't cost much money. You should keep a goldfish in a fish tank, because they need a lot of room to swim. Put small plants in the bottom of the tank. This will make your goldfish very happy. Change your goldfish's water, often. Taking care of a goldfish is much easier than taking care of a dog or cat!

Goldfish are very clever fish. They know different shapes and colors. These little fish make great pets!

1. What color are most goldfish?

   A. black
   B. brown
   C. orange

   This question asks you about information in the story. Look back at the story. What color are most goldfish? The author says that goldfish can be black (answer choice A) or brown (answer choice B), but that is not the color of most fish. The author says that most fish are orange. This makes answer choice C the best choice.

2. How many pounds was the biggest goldfish?

   A. four
   B. nine
   C. fifty

   Look back at the story. The author says that most goldfish are small. But wild goldfish can be quite large. The author says that the largest goldfish weighed nine pounds. This means that answer choice A and C are not correct. Answer choice B is correct.

3. This story shows that the writer most likely feels that goldfish are
   A. not smart.
   B. not pretty.
   C. good pets.

   This question asks you to think about how the write probably feels about goldfish. You can tell how the writer feels by what he or she says. The writer does not say that goldfish are not smart. The writer says they are clever. This means answer choice A is wrong. Answer choice B is also incorrect. The writer never says that goldfish are not pretty. The writer does say that goldfish make good pets. Answer choice C is right.

4. In this story, the word <u>lonely</u> means
   A. sad.
   B. mad.
   C. happy.

   Look at the word. How is it used in the story? The author doesn't want the fish to be *lonely*. The word lonely doesn't mean mad (answer choice A) and it doesn't seem to mean happy (answer choice C). The word *lonely* seems to mean sad. Answer choice A is right.

5. Which sentence is true about goldfish?

   A. They can live in small bowls.
   B. They eat very little food.
   C. They are very easy to care for.

   This question asks you to choose the sentence about goldfish that is true. The writer says that goldfish should not live in small bowls, so answer choice A is not correct. The writer doesn't say that goldfish need very little food. Answer choice B is not correct. The writer does say that goldfish are easy to care for. This means answer choice C is the right answer.

6. Why does the writer call goldfish clever?

   A. Goldfish can see shapes and colors.
   B. Goldfish can swim very far.
   C. Goldfish come in many different colors.

   Why does the writer think that goldfish are clever? The writer does not say that goldfish can swim very far. Answer choice B is not right. Though goldfish can be many colors, this is not why the writer thinks they are clever. Answer choice C is wrong. The writer does think that goldfish are clever because they can see shapes and colors. Answer choice A is the correct answer.

PAINTING A ROOM

Sometimes, people want to change a room. A good way to change a room is with paint. Painting doesn't cost a lot of money and it is easy to do.

First, you need to pick a paint color. Pick a color that you like and won't get tired of. Stay away from dark colors. If you use a dark color, you might be stuck with that color because it is harder to cover. Choose a light color.

Once you choose a color, you buy the paint from a paint store. You also need to gather a paint pan and a paintbrush. Next, you need to get the room ready. To keep from getting paint on the floor, cover the floor with something old. An old sheet works well. Next, use a rag to clean the walls. Paint doesn't stick to dirty walls.

After you are finished cleaning the walls, you can begin to paint. Try not to miss any spots. Do not touch the paint when it's wet, because this will leave a spot on the wall. Keep in mind that the color of wet paint is different from the color of dry paint. So, if your color looks a little too dark when you brush it on, it may change when it dries.

1. How many word parts are in the word COLOR?

   A. 1
   B. 2
   C. 3

   The question asks you to count the number of parts in the word *color*. Read the word again. Count the number of parts or syllables in the word. You can tell it does not have one part (answer choice A) and it does not have three parts (answer choice C). When you read the word, you can count two parts (answer choice B). Answer choice B is the best answer.

2. The story says you should cover the floors with something so

   A. the paint will come off the floor.
   B. the paint will stick to the walls.
   C. the floor does not get paint on it.

   This question asks you to give the reason the floor should be covered. The story says the paint will not come off the floor, so answer choice A is not correct. Covering the floors does not have to do anything with the walls. You can cross off answer choice B. The paint will not get on floor if you cover it. Answer choice C is the best.

3. With what should you use to clean the walls?

   A. a rag
   B. a brush
   C. a pan

   This question wants you to find out what the story says to use to clean the walls. Look at answer choice A. A rag can be used to clean things. Answer choice might be right. Answer choice B is a brush. A brush is used to paint on wall. Answer choice B is not correct. Answer choice C is a pan. A pan is used to hold things, such as paint. Answer choice C is not right. Answer choice A is the best choice.

4. In this story, the word <u>gather</u> means

   A. move.
   B. sell.
   C. collect.

   This question asks you to find the meaning of the word *gather*. The story does not say to move the paint pan and paint brush. Answer choice A isn't a good choice. The story does not say you should sell the paint pan and paint brush. Answer choice B is not right. The story says you should gather a paint pan and a paintbrush. You need to go and get the pan and brush to paint, so gather means to find and bring together, or to collect. This means answer choice C is the best answer.

> Do not touch the paint when <u>it's</u> wet, because this will leave a spot on the wall.

5. <u>It's</u> in this sentence means

   A. is.
   B. it is.
   C. it is not.

   The word it's is a contraction. In a contraction, an apostrophe is used in place of a letter. Answer choice A is not correct, because the word it is part of the contraction. Answer choice B is correct. The contraction it's means it is. Answer choice C is not correct. There is not a contraction for all three of these words.

FROGS

Have you ever seen a frog? If you have, what did it look like? Frogs have <u>long</u> legs and large eyes and feet. Their toes are webbed. This helps them swim. There are many different types and colors of frogs. While many frogs are dull green, others are bright red and yellow. Frogs live almost everywhere. Most frogs live near water, but some live on land. A few kinds of frogs even live in hot deserts!

Frogs have very strong back legs. They use their legs to jump very far. Most frogs jump better than they walk. A few kinds of frogs cannot walk at all. They can only jump or swim.

All frogs lay eggs. Frog eggs are tiny, and most frogs lay hundreds of eggs. These eggs will hatch in about one week. Baby frogs are called tadpoles. Tadpoles look like fish. They don't have legs. They have only fins, a tail, and a head. Tadpoles live in water. Over time, tadpoles grow legs, and crawl out of the water. Then they lose their tails. When this happens, they look like frogs.

Read this sentence from the story.

Frogs have long legs and large eyes and feet.

1. Which word means the opposite of long?

   A. tall
   B. big
   C. short

2. Which word rhymes with frog?

   A. for
   B. log
   C. fresh

3. Where do most frogs live?

   A. in water
   B. in deserts
   C. near water

4. How long does it take for a frog's eggs to hatch?

   A. one day
   B. one week
   C. two weeks

5. What is a baby frog called?

   A. a fish
   B. an egg
   C. a tadpole

6. Have you ever seen a frog? Where did you see it? What did it look like?

THE STAR
by Jane Taylor

Twinkle, twinkle, little star
How I wonder what you are!
Up above the world so high,
Like a diamond in the sky.

When the blazing sun is gone,
When he nothing shines upon,
Then you show your little light,
Twinkle, twinkle, all the night.

Then the traveler in the <u>dark,</u>
Thanks you for your tiny spark,
He could not see which way to go,
If you did not twinkle so.

In the dark blue sky you keep,
And often through my curtains peep,
For you never shut your eye,
Till the sun is in the sky.

As your bright and tiny spark,

Lights the traveler in the dark-

Though I know not what you are,

Twinkle, twinkle, little star.

1. Which word rhymes with <u>dark</u>?

    A. dirt
    B. cart
    C. mark

2. When does the star shut its eye?

    A. when the sun is in the sky
    B. when it shows its little light
    C. when it is up above the world so high

3. Which word has the same ending sound as EYE?

    A. by
    B. me
    C. eel

4. How does the star help the traveler?

    A. by making it warm
    B. my shining up high
    C. by making it bright

"If you did not twinkle so."

5. Which word has two word parts?

   A. you
   B. did
   C. twinkle

6. What do stars look like in the sky? What do you think about when you look at them?

THE ANT AND THE GRASSHOPPER
adapted from Aesop's fable

Once upon a time there lived an Ant and a Grasshopper. One summer day, Grasshopper was having fun hopping about. While he was playing, he saw Ant working hard to carry an ear of corn back to his nest.

"Why don't you stop working and play with me?" asked Grasshopper.

"I can't," <u>replied</u> Ant. I need to gather food for the winter. If I don't work now, I will be sorry later. You should also work to make sure you have enough food for the winter."

Grasshopper thought Ant was foolish. There was plenty of food to eat now. Why should he worry about the winter? Why should he waste time working when he would rather sing and play?

Grasshopper changed his mind, however, when the air grew cold and snow covered the ground. He searched and searched, but he could not find food anywhere. He was just about to give up and die of hunger when he had an idea. He would visit Ant and beg for something to eat.

Ant was happy to see his friend and he let him eat until he could eat no more. He knew that Grasshopper had learned an important lesson: It is always a good idea to plan ahead.

1. Another good title for this story would be

   A. "Planning Ahead."
   B. "Eating Good Food."
   C. "Playing in Summer."

2. Grasshopper was hungry during the winter because he

   A. did not know how to find food in winter.
   B. could not find his friend Ant.
   C. did not save food during the summer.

3. This story is make-believe because

   A. an Ant finds food to eat.
   B. an Ant and a Grasshopper talk.
   C. a Grasshopper likes to hop.

4. Which sentence is true about Ant?

   A. He is smart.
   B. He is mean.
   C. He is fun.

Read this sentence from the story.

> " I can't," replied Ant.

5. What does the word replied mean?

   A. said
   B. shouted
   C. asked

MAKING BANANA BREAD

Ingredients:

2 eggs

1 3/4 cup sifted flour

2 teaspoon baking powder

1/4 teaspoon baking soda

1/2 teaspoon salt

1/3 cup vegetable oil

2/3 cup sugar

1 cup mashed bananas

1. Ask a grown-up to heat the oven.
2. Mash bananas with a fork in a <u>small</u> bowl.
3. Beat eggs in another bowl.
4. In a large, bowl mix together flour, baking powder, baking soda, and salt.
5. Add the vegetable oil to the large bowl.
6. Stir sugar into large bowl. Continue stirring until the mix is fluffy.

7. Add the eggs to the large bowl.

8. Add flour and bananas. Stir well.

9. Bake for 70 minutes.

10. Let bread cool. Then slice and enjoy!

Makes 16 slices.

1. How many ingredients does the recipe need?
    A. 4
    B. 6
    C. 8

2. How much sugar do you need to make the banana bread?
    A. 1/2 teaspoon
    B. 2/3 cup
    C. 1/3 cup

3. How much banana bread does this recipe make?
    A. 2 slices
    B. 8 slices
    C. 16 slices

> Beat eggs in another bowl.

4. Which word has three word parts?

   A. beat
   B. another
   C. eggs

5. Which word has the same ending sound as the word <u>small</u>?

   A. tall
   B. smart
   C. sugar

6. What other ingredients might be good in the banana bread? Name two things you would add to the bread.

ROBIN

The robin is probably the best-known bird in the United States. It can often be seen searching city lawns for insects and earthworms. A robin is about eight to nine inches long. Both the adult male and adult female have orange-red breasts and gray backs.

A robin's nest is usually a thick, round-shaped bowl. It is made of mud, twigs, and leaves. It is often lined with <u>soft</u> grass. Nests can be found in any kind of tree or on a building.

Four or five greenish-blue eggs make up a "brood." The robin usually has two broods a season.

Robins go south during the winter months. When they return from their winter homes, it is a sign of the start of spring. Keep an eye on your lawn or sit in a city park. You will be able to watch the robins as they search for food.

1. Which sentence is true about robins?

   A. Only male robins have orange-red breasts.
   B. Robins are one of the best-known birds.
   C. Only female robins look for food.

2. A robin's nest is usually shaped like a

   A. fork.
   B. spoon.
   C. bowl.

3. The robin's nest is lined with

   A. grass.
   B. twigs.
   C. leaves.

4. Which word means the opposite of the word <u>soft</u>?

   A. above
   B. hard
   C. kick

5. Where would you most likely see a robin?

   A. on a lawn
   B. on a street
   C. in a house

6. Robins go south during the

   A. summer
   B. spring
   C. winter

THE BEAR FACTS

In some places, it is against the law to feed bears. Human food can kill a bear. A human-fed bear lives for only eight years. A bear in the wild lives for about 12 years.

Some bears lose their natural fears of people. These bears can be dangerous. Sometimes they need to be destroyed. For their sake and yours, please do not feed the bears or other wildlife.

At the beginning of the summer, a male bear weighs about 250 pounds. Females are a little over 100 pounds. However, they may be twice as big by the fall. Bears, like humans, are "omnivores." That means they will eat both plants and animals. They eat mostly plants. They get most of their protein from insects. Sometimes they eat small animals.

Most bears enter a deep sleep starting in late fall. Cubs are born in January. Newborns and mothers <u>remain</u> in their dens until April. Cubs remain with their mothers for a year and a half.

1. Why did the writer write this story?

    A. to tell what most bears look like
    B. to ask people not to feed bears
    C. to tell people not to chase bears

2. Human-fed bears do not

    A. live as long as wild bears.
    B. eat enough good food.
    C. sleep during the winter.

| Human food can kill a bear. |

3. Which word has two word parts?

    A. food
    B. human
    C. bear

4. What do bears mostly eat?

    A. plants
    B. bugs
    C. animals

5. People should not feed bears because bears
   A. will gain weight.
   B. can harm people.
   C. will not eat plants.

Read this sentence from the story.

> Newborns and mothers <u>remain</u> in their dens until April.

6. Which word means the same as the word <u>remain</u>?
   A. stay
   B. live
   C. stand

THE HOUSE SPARROW

You have probably seen a house sparrow. This little bird is common all over the United States. The house sparrow is about six inches long and has a thick beak. In the country, house sparrows nest in the same places as bluebirds. This means that they live very close to bluebirds. In the city, house sparrows live near people. They might nest in a bush near a house. Large numbers of house sparrows sometimes rest, or roost, together at night. House sparrows eat mostly seeds, but they also eat bugs.

During the spring, summer, and late fall, house sparrows built their nests. They make their nests from grass, string, and anything else that they can pick up. They lay their eggs in their nests. And when the eggs hatch, they care for their babies. They usually have four to six babies at a time.

1. House sparrows usually eat

   A. grass.
   B. seeds.
   C. eggs.

2. Where do house sparrows in cities live?

   A. in trees
   B. near bluebirds
   C. near people

3. How big is a house sparrow?

   A. 6 inches
   B. 8 inches
   C. 10 inches

4. How many babies do house sparrows usually have at one time?

   A. 1–2 babies
   B. 4–6 babies
   C. 7–9 babies

5. Which word means the opposite of <u>thick</u>?

   A. light
   B. thin
   C. large

IGGY

Andy had wanted a pet of his own for a long time. Now that he was in second grade, his father said he was <u>old</u> enough for a pet. Andy's friend Rico had a cute dog. His friend Amy had a cat, and his friend Lilly had a bird that liked to sing. But Andy <u>didn't</u> want a dog, a cat, or a bird. He wanted a different kind of pet. He had seen this kind of pet in a pet store.

When Saturday came, Andy's dad took him to the pet store. Andy showed his dad the pet he wanted. "I guess so, Andy," his father said. "But that pet doesn't have fur. And it's not even cute." "I think he's very cute. He's an iguana, a kind of lizard. I'll call him Iggy," said Andy with a smile.

1. This story is about

    A. a boy who wants a different kind of pet.
    B. a father who lets a boy get a pet.
    C. a boy who has a really cute dog.

But Andy <u>didn't</u> want a dog, a cat, or a bird.

2. <u>Didn't</u> in this sentence means

    A. not.
    B. did no.
    C. did not.

Andy showed his dad the pet he wanted.

3. Which word has two word parts?

    A. dad
    B. pet
    C. showed

4. What did Andy want to name his pet?

    A. Iggy
    B. Liz
    C. Rico

Read this sentence from the story.

> Now that he was in second grade, his father said he was <u>old</u> enough for a pet.

5. Which word means the opposite of <u>old</u>?

    A. big
    B. young
    C. last

6. Andy's friend Lilly has a pet

    A. dog.
    B. cat.
    C. bird.

7. What kind of pet would you like to have? Explain your answer.

THE COW
by Robert Louis Stevenson

The friendly cow, all red and white,

I love with all my heart:

She gives me cream with all her might,

To eat with apple tart.

She wanders lowing here and there,

And yet she cannot stray,

All in the pleasant open air,

The pleasant light of day;

And blown by all the winds that pass

And wet with all the <u>showers</u>,

She walks among the meadow grass

And eats the meadow flowers.

1. This poem is mostly about

   A. a cow.
   B. a tart.
   C. some flowers.

2. Which word has the same ending sound as the word PASS?

   A. put
   B. grass
   C. flowers

3. Which sentence is true about the cow?

   A. She is sad.
   B. She is nice.
   C. She is small.

4. In this poem, the word <u>showers</u> means

   A. to rain.
   B. to wash.
   C. to drink.

5. What does the cow eat?

   A. grass
   B. cream
   C. flowers

6. How do you think the speaker of the poem feels about the cow? Why?

THE OLYMPICS

Every four years the Olympics are held in a different place. People from all over the world come to watch the competitors in the Olympics. Competitors are people who try to win. Some competitors in the Olympics try to be the fastest runner. Others try to be the strongest. Some try to jump the highest. The winners met medals made of gold, silver, and bronze. The first-place winner gets a gold medal.

If you are good at a sport, you might enter the Olympics <u>one</u> day. It takes a lot of work to be good enough for the Olympics. The best thing about the Olympics is that people try their hardest to be the best at a sport that they love to play.

1. When are the Olympics held?

   A. every year
   B. every two years
   C. every four years

2. Which word has the same ending sound as FASTEST?

   A. face
   B. biggest
   C. last

Read this sentence from the story.

> If you are good at a sport, you might enter the Olympics <u>one</u> day.

3. Which word sounds the same as <u>one</u>?

   A. won
   B. only
   C. sun

4. A first-place winner in the Olympics gets a medal made of

   A. bronze
   B. silver
   C. gold

5. Would you like to be in the Olympics someday? Why or why not?

THE BALD EAGLE

The bald eagle is the national symbol of the United States. This means that the bald eagle stands for the United States. People made the bald eagle the symbol of the United States many years ago on June 20, 1782. Benjamin Franklin, one of the founding fathers of the United States, did not want the bald eagle to be a symbol. He thought the turkey should be the symbol of the United States. But other people thought turkeys did not look nice. They thought the bald eagle was a better symbol.

Bald eagles are beautiful birds. They have snow-white feathers on their heads and tails. Their white heads make them look bald. They have brown and black feathers on their bodies. Their bill, eyes, and feet are bright yellow. The females are larger than the males, but the males are still very big.

The bald eagle builds a huge nest. It can be seven or eight feet wide. This is taller than a person! A bald eagle's nest is made of sticks and has fine grass or moss inside to make it soft. Bald eagles build their nests very high in trees.

1. What bird did Benjamin Franklin want to be the symbol of the United States?

   A. the turkey
   B. the chicken
   C. the eagle

2. Which word rhymes with <u>well</u>?

   A. fall
   B. fell
   C. full

3. What color is the bald eagle's head?

   A. brown
   B. yellow
   C. white

4. What part of a bald eagle is bright yellow?

   A. its body
   B. its feet
   C. its tail

5. In this story, the word <u>huge</u> means

   A. tall.
   B. big.
   C. heavy.

6. Do you think the bald eagle is a good symbol of our country? Why or why not?

   _____
   _____
   _____
   _____
   _____
   _____
   _____
   _____
   _____
   _____
   _____
   _____

PLANTING A FLOWER GARDEN

Many people like having flowers near their homes. You can plant flowers near your home, too. You can make a flower garden.

First, get a can filled with water, some flower seeds, and a small shovel. Then, ask a grownup to help you find a piece of ground in which you can dig. Next, use the shovel to dig a small hole in the ground. Do not make the hole too deep. Put one of the flower seed in the hole. Then, cover the seed with dirt. Next, water the seed with water from the can.

After planting the seed, look at it every day. Give the seed water if the ground is dry. Also, make sure the seed gets sunlight. Sunlight, water, and air will help the seed to grow. Soon, you should see a small, green plant growing in the dirt. Look at the plant every day and give it water, too. If you take care of the plant, it will grow larger.

When the plant is large, it will grow flowers. At first, the flowers will be very small. Then, the flowers will grow big. Next, they will open up. When the flowers open, you will have a beautiful flower garden.

1. In this story, the word <u>dirt</u> means

    A. green grass.
    B. water.
    C. loose ground.

2. What should do before you put the seed in the ground?

    A. dig a hole
    B. cover a hole
    C. water the seed

3. How many word parts are there in the word FLOWERS?

    A. 1
    B. 2
    C. 3

4. What helps the seed grow?

    A. sunlight
    B. food
    C. flowers

5. Which word rhymes with <u>care</u>?

   A. cart
   B. cup
   C. bear

6. What happens before a plant gets flowers?

   A. It gets seeds.
   B. It grows big.
   C. It opens up.

SUMMER ALL YEAR LONG

Kate liked the summer. She liked the warm air and sunshine. In the summer, she swam. She also rode her bike. The summer was about to end. Kate was not happy. She wanted the summer to last all year long.

Kate and her mother went for a <u>walk</u>. They looked at the trees. The leaves were about to change colors.

"I do want the leaves to change. I want it to be summer all year long," said Kate.

"The leaves will turn yellow, orange, and red. They will be beautiful," said her mother.

"I want everything to stay the <u>same</u>," said Kate.

"We would not like summer if it stayed all year long," said her mother.

Kate thought about what her mother said. She knew her mother was right. Summer all year long would not be exciting.

In a week, the leaves were no longer green. They were yellow, orange, and red. Kate liked looking at leaves. They were <u>beautiful</u>. Then, the leaves began to fall from the trees. Kate made a pile of leaves. She jumped into the pile. The leaves flew into the air. Kate laughed. She did not want summer all year long.

1. Which word rhymes with walk?

   A. talk
   B. week
   C. sick

Read this sentence from the story.

> "I want everything to stay the same," said Kate.

2. Which word means the opposite of same?

   A. alike
   B. warm
   C. different

3. What does Kate's mother like about fall?

   A. the cool air
   B. the things you can do
   C. the color of the leaves

4. This story is mostly about a girl who likes

   A. to ride bikes.
   B the summer.
   C. look at leaves.

5. In this story, the word <u>beautiful</u> means

   A. strange.
   B. pretty.
   C. funny.

6. What does Kate do after she makes a pile of leaves?

   A. rides her bike
   B. jumps in the leaves
   C. looks at the leaves

AWESOME ADVENTURES

Mountain Workshops is a camp that offers trips for kids. Kids of all ages can <u>enjoy</u> our trips.

Are you ready to go canoeing? Hiking? Rock climbing? Caving? Kayaking? Would you like to build a raft? Try something new? Make new friends? Play hard? Get dirty? Laugh and play together?

If you can't decide what you want to do the most, Awesome Adventure Day Programs are perfect for you! We do it all! Our day programs run Monday through Friday, 8:00 a.m. to 4:00 p.m. They feature a new adventure each day. We meet at a place close to where you live. Your parents can bring you there. Then we go off on different trips. However, you don't just ride in a bus. You get out and do great things almost all day!

Our Awesome Adventures Biking Day Programs give you a chance to try biking in new locations in the area. You will learn tons of great stuff. You will learn about how to care for your bike and how to bike safely on the trail or on the road. You will learn to become a stronger biker.

You will enjoy some the greatest biking spots in our area. You will bike with instructors who love biking and can't wait for you to love it, too. You should bring your own bike, helmet, lunch, and water every day.

1. This story is mostly about
    A. how to care for your bike.
    B. a biking program.
    C. the best places to bike ride.

2. In this story, the word <u>enjoy</u> means
    A. like.
    B. move.
    C. give.

3. What will you learn on your day trip?
    A. how bikes are made
    B. how to bike safely
    C. how bikes work

4. What should you bring with you every day?

   A. a book
   B. a friend
   C. your lunch

5. What is different each day you go biking?

   A. the people who teach you
   B. the spots where you bike
   C. the place that you meet

6. Would you rather do something every day or go biking every day? Why?

TRAFFIC

There is too much traffic on our highways. A 20-mile trip will take 20 minutes with no cars on the roads. During rush hour, the same trip will take over an hour.

Everyone agrees that something has to be done. No one likes to spend that much time going to work. Going home can take even longer.

We cannot build more highways. There is no room. They are very expensive. There is not enough money.

Many people believe that the answer is to get more people to take trains. However, there is not enough parking at the train stations now. We can build new parking lots. We can build new parking garages. We can even build new train stations with lots of new parking. Nevertheless, the trains are already too crowded. There is no money for more trains.

Suppose we could get more trains. It really would not make that much difference in the number of cars on the road.

Trucks are a problem, too. Trucks are big. They go fast. They can be dangerous. There are so many on the road. They make the traffic much worse.

Some people think the answer is freight trains. If more freight went on trains, less would have to go on the highways. However, freight trains must be loaded and unloaded. Trucks would still have to pick up and deliver most goods.

There is no <u>easy</u> solution to the traffic problem. Traffic will probably trouble us for a long time.

1. Traffic is a problem because there are too many
   A. cars.
   B. trains.
   C. roads.

2. Which word means the opposite of <u>easy</u>?
   A. simple
   B. hard
   C. old

3. Another good title for this passage would be

   A. "Building New Roads."
   B. "Getting to Work on Time."
   C. "Finding a Place to Park."

4. Many people that traffic will go away if more people rode to work in

   A. cars.
   B. trucks.
   C. trains.

5. Which word has the same ending sound as PARKING?

   A. rock.
   B. proud
   C. looking

6. How do you think the author of this passage feels about traffic? Why?

THE RAT PRINCESS

Once upon a time, there was a Rat Princess. She lived with her father, the Rat King, and her mother, the Rat Queen, in a rice field in faraway Japan. The Rat Princess was so pretty that her father and mother were quite foolishly proud of her. They thought no one was good enough to play with her. When she grew up, they would not let any of the rat princes come to visit her. They decided at last that no one should marry her till they had found the most powerful person in the whole world. No one else was good enough. Soon, the Father Rat started out to find the most powerful person in the whole world.

The wisest and oldest rat in the rice field said that the Sun must be the most powerful person because he made the rice grow and ripen. So the Rat King went to find the Sun. He climbed up the highest mountain, ran up the path of a rainbow, and traveled across the sky till he came to the Sun's house.

"What do you want, little brother?" the Sun said, when he saw him.

"I come," said the Rat King, very importantly, "to offer you the hand of my daughter, the princess, because you are the most powerful person in the world. No one else is good enough."

"Ha, ha!" laughed the jolly round Sun and winked his eye. "You are very kind, little brother, but if that is the case then the princess is not for me. The Cloud is more powerful than I am. When he passes over me, I cannot shine."

"Oh, indeed," said the Rat King, "then you are not my man at all." He left the Sun. The Sun laughed and winked to himself.

The Rat King traveled across the sky till he came to the Cloud's house.

"What do you want, little brother?" sighed the Cloud when he saw him.

"I come to offer you the hand of my daughter, the princess," said the Rat King, "because you are the most powerful person in the world. The Sun said so and no one else is good enough."

The Cloud sighed again. "I am not the most powerful person," he said. "The Wind is stronger than I am. When he blows, I have to go wherever he sends me."

"Then you are not the person for my daughter," said the Rat King proudly. He started at once to find the Wind. He traveled across the sky, till he came at last to the Wind's house, at the very edge of the world.

When the Wind saw him coming, he laughed a big, gusty laugh. "Ho, ho!" he said. The Wind asked the Rat King what he wanted. When the Rat King told him that he had come to offer him the Rat Princess's hand because he was the most powerful person in the world, the Wind shouted a great gusty shout. He said, "No, no, I am not the strongest. The Wall that man has made is stronger than I. I cannot make him move, with all my blowing. Go to the Wall, little brother!"

And the Rat King climbed down the sky-path again, and traveled across the earth till he came to the Wall. It was quite near his own rice field.

"What do you want, little brother?" grumbled the Wall when he saw him.

"I come to offer you the hand of the princess, my daughter, because you are the most powerful person in the world. No one else is good enough."

"Ugh, ugh," grumbled the Wall. "I am not the strongest. The big gray Rat who lives in the cellar is stronger than I. When he gnaws and gnaws at me, I crumble and crumble until at last I fall. Go to the Rat, little brother."

And so, after going all over the world to find the strongest person, the Rat King had to marry his daughter to a rat after all. However, the princess was very glad of it, for she wanted to marry the Gray Rat all the time.

1. The Rat King thought his daughter was

   A. pretty.
   B. kind.
   C. wise.

2. The Rat King want his daughter to marry someone with

   A. money.
   B. power.
   C. dreams.

3. Who does the Rat King go to see first?

   A. the wind
   B. the cloud
   C. the sun

4. In this story, the word <u>jolly</u> means

   A. happy.
   B. foolish.
   C. daring.

5. This story is make-believe because

   A. the animals can talk.
   B. the wind blows the cloud.
   C. the rat gnaws at the wall.

6. At the end of the story, the princess is happy because

   A. her father returned home.
   B. she was given a gift.
   C. she married the Gray Rat.

JENNY WREN ARRIVES

It was very early in the morning. In fact, jolly, bright Mr. Sun had hardly begun his daily climb up in the blue, blue sky. It was nothing <u>unusual</u> for Peter Rabbit to see jolly Mr. Sun get up in the morning. It would be more unusual for Peter not to see him, for you know Peter likes to stay out all night.

Peter had been out all night this time, but he wasn't at all sleepy. You see, sweet Mistress Spring had arrived. There was so much happening on every side. Peter was so afraid that he would miss something that he wouldn't have slept at all if he could have helped it. Peter had come over to the Old Orchard early this morning to see if there had been any new arrivals the day before.

"Birds are funny creatures," said Peter, as he hopped over a low place in the old stone wall and was fairly in the Old Orchard.

"Tut, tut, tut, tut, tut!" cried a rather sharp scolding voice. "Tut, tut, tut, tut, tut! You don't know what you are talking about, Peter Rabbit. They are not funny creatures at all. They are the most sensible folks in all the wide world."

Peter cut a long hop short right in the middle, to sit up with shining eyes. "Oh, Jenny Wren, I'm so glad to see you! When did you arrive?" he cried.

"Mr. Wren and I have just arrived. Thank goodness we are here at last," replied Jenny Wren. She was fussing about, as only she can, in a <u>branch</u> above Peter. "I never was more thankful in my life to see a place than I am right this minute to see the Old Orchard once more. It seems ages and ages since we left it."

"Well, if you are so fond of it, what did you leave it for?" demanded Peter. "It is just as I said before—you birds are funny creatures. You never stay put; at least a lot of you don't. Sammy Jay and Tommy Tit the Chickadee and Drummer the Woodpecker and a few others have a little sense; they don't go off on long, foolish journeys. But the rest of you—"

"Tut, tut, tut, tut, tut!" interrupted Jenny Wren. "You don't know what you are talking about. No one sounds so silly as one who tries to talk about something he knows nothing about."

Peter chuckled. "That tongue of yours is just as sharp as ever," said he. "But just the same it is good to hear it. We certainly would miss it. I was beginning to be a little worried for fear something might have happened to you so that you wouldn't be back here this summer. You know me well enough, Jenny Wren, to know that you can't hurt me with your tongue, sharp as it is. So you may as well save your breath to tell me a few things I want to know. Now if you are as fond of the Old Orchard as you pretend to be, why did you ever leave it?"

Jenny Wren's bright eyes snapped. "Why do you eat?" she asked tartly.

"Because I'm hungry," replied Peter promptly.

"What would you eat if there were nothing to eat?" snapped Jenny.

"That's a silly question," retorted Peter.

"No more silly than asking me why I leave the Old Orchard," replied Jenny. "Do give us birds credit for a little common sense, Peter. We can't live without eating any more than you can. In winter, there is no food at all here for most of us, so we go where there is food. Those who are lucky enough to eat the kinds of food that can be found here in winter stay here. They are lucky. That's what they are—lucky. Still . . . " Jenny Wren paused.

"Still what?" prompted Peter.

"I wonder sometimes if you folks who are at home all the time know just what a blessed place home is," replied Jenny. "It is only six months since we went south, but I said it seems ages, and it does. The best part of going away is coming home. I don't care if that does sound rather mixed; it is true just the same. It isn't home down there in the sunny South, even if we do spend as much time there as we do here. THIS is home, and there's no place like it! What's that, Mr. Wren? I haven't seen all the Great World? Perhaps I haven't, but I've seen enough of it, let me tell you that! Anyone who travels a thousand miles twice a year as we do has a right to express an opinion, especially if they have used their eyes as I have mine. There is no place like home, and you needn't try to tease me by pretending that there is. My dear, I know you; you are just as tickled to be back here as I am."

"He sings as if he were," said Peter, for all the time Mr. Wren was singing with all his might.

Jenny Wren looked over at Mr. Wren fondly. "Isn't he a dear to sing to me like that? And isn't it a perfectly beautiful spring song?" said she. Then, without waiting for Peter to reply, her tongue rattled on. "I do wish he would be careful. Sometimes I am afraid he will overdo. Just look at him now! He is singing so hard that he is shaking all over. He always is that way. There is one thing true about us Wrens, and this is that when we do things we do them with all our might. When we work, we work with all our might. When Mr. Wren sings, he sings with all his might."

"And, when you scold, you scold with all your might," interrupted Peter mischievously.

Jenny Wren opened her mouth for a sharp reply, but laughed instead. "I suppose I do scold a good deal," said she, "but if I didn't, goodness knows who wouldn't impose on us. I can't bear to be imposed on. But gracious, Peter Rabbit, I can't sit here all day talking to you! I must find out who else has arrived in the Old Orchard and must look my old house over to see if it is fit to live in."

1. In this story, the word <u>unusual</u> means

   A. strange.
   B. scary.
   C. sleepy.

2. Why isn't Peter Rabbit sleepy?

   A. He slept long enough.
   B. Spring had arrived.
   C. The sun is very bright.

3. Who yells at Peter Rabbit?

   A. Mr. Sun
   B. Mr. Wren
   C. Jenny Wren

4. Which word has the same ending sound as the word <u>branch</u>?

   A. ranch
   B. enough
   C. round

5. Another good title for this story would be

   A. "Good Friends"
   B. "Spring Has Sprung"
   C. "A New Home"

6. Mr. Wren trembles when he sings because he is

   A. afraid of Mrs. Wren's scolding.
   B. tired from his long flight.
   C. singing with all his might.

WETLAND: MORE THAN JUST A SWAMP

Wetlands are very important. What are these areas and what do they do? A wetland is the area between dry land and open water. It is sometimes covered with a shallow layer of water. There are also wetlands that can be dry for part of the year. There are many different kinds of wetlands.

Some Kinds of Wetland

Swamp: Some wetlands are flooded throughout most of the year. Trees and shrubs still grow <u>there</u>. They are considered swamp.

Bottomland: These are the lowlands along streams and rivers. They have both wet and dry periods during the year. Bottomlands often have trees growing on them.

Marsh: Marshes are wet areas filled with grasses and rushes. Marshes can be found in freshwater areas. They also are in saltwater areas near the ocean.

Wetland Functions:

Flood Control: Wetland plants slow down the flow of water from heavy rains. The water is stored in the low-lying areas of wetlands. This prevents the water from flowing into nearby rivers and streams. If it did, they would flood and damage property.

Storm Buffer: Along our coasts, wetlands take a beating from high winds and waves. They are not damaged. The thick growth of plants makes the force of storms less harmful. It also protects the land from erosion.

Water Banks: Wetlands hold water during the wet season. This water seeps through the soil into our underground water supplies.

Water Filter: Wetlands help clean waters that carry pollutants. Silt and soil fall to the bottom of the wetlands. Otherwise they would harm life in the water. Wastes are broken down and absorbed by plants. So are many harmful chemicals.

Nurseries: Many fish and animals use wetlands as places to bring up their young. They provide an abundant supply of food and shelter for the young.

Home Sweet Home: Wetlands are home to many animals. A thriving wetland probably has more life in it than any other kind of habitat.

Wildlife Pantry: Wetlands produce lots of food. Many animals depend on them for food. Many migrating birds stop over in wetlands each spring and fall. They rest and feed before continuing their trip. Some will spend the winter in the wetlands.

Recreational Opportunities: Wetlands provide us with places to watch birds and animals. We also fish, boat, and hunt in wetlands.

Economics: Fisherman know that the wetlands supply us with crabs and many other types of seafood.

1. Which wetland is near the ocean?

   A. swamp
   B. bottomland
   C. marsh

   What are these areas and what do they do?

2. Which word has two word parts?

   A. what
   B. areas
   C. they

3. Which wetland can sometimes be dry?

   A. swamp
   B. bottomland
   C. marsh

4. How do wetlands help people?

   A. They give people water to drink.
   B. They slow down the flow of water.
   C. They help people travel down river.

5. How do wetlands clean the water?

   A. plants break down wastes
   B. water carries waste away
   C. winds blow wastes away

Read this sentence from the story.

> Trees and shrubs still grow there.

6. Which word sounds like the word there?

   A. their
   B. think
   C. this

THE GOLDEN FINGERS

Once upon a time, there was a king who lived at the bottom of a very tall hill. On top of the hill there was a magic pot of gold. It was guarded by two golden fingers. They were big, strong, and mean-looking.

One day, the king ran out of gold. He thought it would be a good idea to get some gold from the top of the hill. The king did not want to go himself. He thought it might be dangerous.

So the king called his advisors to his throne. "Whom should I send to get the gold at the top of the hill?" he said.

The advisors were the smartest men and women in the land. They said, "Send the bravest men."

The bravest men in the castle were knights. One by one, the king sent each of the knights in the castle. Each knight rode up the hill. When each of the knights reached the golden fingers, the fingers closed. The knights could not get to the gold.

The king called his advisors again. "The knights failed," he said. "Who should I send now?"

The advisors said. "Send the richest men. They know how to get gold."

The king decided to send the nobles. They were the richest men in the land. They were not very brave, but when the king ordered them to go, they went. The fingers would not let any of the nobles near the gold either.

The only people left in the castle were the pages. They were training to be knights. They were still quite young. The king really, really wanted the gold, so he decided to send the pages. They rode to the top of the hill. When they got to the top of the hill, the golden fingers opened wide for them. They got the pot of gold. They took the gold to the happy king.

The king wrote a letter to his children. In it he said, "Remember, if you ever need gold, let your pages do the walking through the yellow fingers."

1. This story is make-believe because

   A. there is a magic pot of gold.
   B. the king ran out of gold.
   C. there are knights at the castle.

2. Another good title for this story would be

   A. "The Page's Problem."
   B. "The King's Gold."
   C. "The Nobles Fight."

3. Who did the kind send up the hill first?

   A. the advisors
   B. the pages
   C. the knights

4. The richest men in the kingdom were the

   A. nobles.
   B. pages.
   C. knights.

5. The golden fingers opened for the

   A. king.
   B. pages.
   C. nobles.

6. Which word means the opposite of <u>failed</u>?

   A. ran
   B. sat
   C. won

WHY THE MORNING GLORY CLIMBS

Once the Morning Glory plant was flat on the ground. She grew that way. She had never climbed at all. Up in the top of a tree near her lived a mother wren and her little baby wren. The little wren was lame. He had a broken wing and couldn't fly. He stayed in the nest all day.

When the mother wren came flying home at night, she told him all about what she saw in the world. One thing she told him about was the beautiful Morning Glory she saw on the ground. She told him about the Morning Glory every day. At last the little wren was filled with a desire to see the Morning Glory for himself.

"How I wish I could see the Morning Glory!" he said.

The Morning Glory heard this. She knew the wren could not see much from his nest. She longed to let the little wren see her face. She decided that she would try to get near enough to let the little Wren see her.

She pulled herself along the ground, a little at a time. Finally she was at the foot of the tree where the little wren lived. But she could not get any farther. She did not know how to climb. She wanted to go up so much that she caught hold of the bark of the tree and pulled herself up a little. And little by little, before she knew it, she was climbing.

And she climbed right up the tree to the little wren's nest. She put her sweet face over the edge of the nest, where the little wren could see.

That was how the Morning Glory came to climb.

1. Where did Morning Glory live?
   A. in a tree
   B. on the ground
   C. in the water

2. The baby bird could not fly because
   A. he hurt his wing.
   B. he was too small.
   C. he felt afraid.

3. What did the mother wren do when she came home?
   A. tell her baby about the world
   B. bring her baby food to eat
   C. care for her baby's hurt wing

4. This story is make-believe because

   A. the birds live in a nest.
   B. the morning glory climbs.
   C. the animals can speak.

5. What did the baby wren hope to do?

   A. learn how to fly
   B. fix his wing
   C. see the Morning Glory

6. What can you tell about Morning Glory from the story?

   A. She is sad.
   B. She is old.
   C. She is kind.

7. Why did Morning Glory climb?

THE PIG BROTHER

There was once a child who was untidy. He left his books on the floor and his muddy shoes on the table. He put his fingers in the jam pots, and spilled ink on his best shirt. There was really no end to his untidiness.

One day the Tidy Fairy came into his room.

"This will never do!" said the fairy. "This is really shocking. You must go out and stay with your brother while I set things to rights here."

"I have no brother!" said the child.

"Yes, you have," said the fairy. "You may not know him, but he will know you. Go out in the garden and watch for him. He will soon come."

"I don't know what you mean!" said the child. The child did not know what to do. Finally, he decided to do what the fairy had said. So he went out into the garden and waited.

Presently a squirrel came along, whisking his tail.

"Are you my brother?" asked the child.

The squirrel looked him over carefully.

"Well, I should hope not!" he said. "My fur is neat and smooth. My nest is handsomely made and in perfect order. My young ones are properly brought up. Why do you insult me by asking such a question?"

He ran off and the child waited.

Presently, a wren came hopping by.

"Are you my brother?" asked the child.

"No, indeed!" said the wren. "What disrespect! You will find no tidier person than I in the whole garden. Not a feather is out of place, and my eggs are the wonder of all for smoothness and beauty. Brother, indeed!" He hopped off, ruffling his feathers, and the child waited.

By and by, a large Tommy Cat came along.

"Are you my brother?" asked the child.

"Go and look at yourself in the glass," said the Tommy Cat haughtily, "and you will have your answer. I have been washing myself in the sun all the morning, while it is clear that no water has come near you for a long time. There are no such creatures as you in my family, I am humbly thankful to say."

He walked on, waving his tail, and the child waited.

Presently, a pig came trotting along.

The child did not wish to ask the pig if he were his brother, but the pig did not wait to be asked.

"Hallo, brother!" he grunted.

"I am not your brother!" said the child.

"Oh yes, you are!" said the pig. "I confess I am not proud of you, but there is no mistaking the members of our family. Come along, and have a good roll in the barnyard! There is some lovely black mud there."

"I don't like to roll in mud!" said the child.

"Tell that to the hens!" said the Pig Brother. "Look at your hands, your shoes, and your shirt! Come along, I say! You may have some of the pig-wash for supper, if there is more than I want."

"I don't want pig-wash!" said the child, and he began to cry.

Just then, the Tidy Fairy came out.

"I have set everything to rights," she said, "and so it must stay. Now, will you go with the Pig Brother, or will you come back with me, and be a tidy child?"

"With you, with you!" cried the child, and he clung to the Fairy's dress.

The Pig Brother grunted. "Small loss!" he said. "There will be all the more pig-wash for me!" And he trotted off.

1. This story is about

    A. an untidy boy.
    B. a good fairy.
    C. a large farm.

Read this sentence from the story

> There was once a child who was untidy.

2. Which word has two parts?

    A. once
    B. was
    C. untidy

3. This story is make-believe because

    A. the boy spilled ink.
    B. the pig rolls in mud.
    C. there is a tidy fairy.

4. Which animal is the boy's brother?

   A. the wren
   B. the cat
   C. the pig

5. When the boy asks if the wren is his brother, the wren feels

   A. nice.
   B. angry.
   C. pretty.

6. What lesson does this story teach?

   _____
   _____
   _____
   _____
   _____
   _____
   _____
   _____
   _____
   _____

WHY THE EVERGREEN TREES KEEP THEIR LEAVES IN WINTER

One day a long, long time ago, it was very cold. Winter was coming and all the birds flew away to the warm south to wait for the spring. However, one little bird had a broken wing and could not fly. He did not know what to do. He looked all around to see if there was any place where he could keep warm. He saw the trees of the great forest.

"Perhaps the trees will keep me warm through the winter," he said.

So he went to the edge of the forest, hopping and fluttering with his broken wing. The first tree he came to was a slim silver birch.

"Beautiful Birch Tree," he said, "will you let me live in your warm branches until the springtime comes?"

"Dear me!" said the birch tree, "What a thing to ask! I have to take care of my own leaves through the winter; that is enough for me. Go away."

The little bird hopped and fluttered with his broken wing until he came to the next tree. It was a great, big oak tree.

"O, Big Oak Tree," said the little bird, "will you let me live in your warm branches until the springtime comes?"

"Dear me," said the oak tree, "What a thing to ask! If you stay in my branches all winter, you will be eating my acorns. Go away."

So the little bird hopped and fluttered with his broken wing till he came to the willow tree by the edge of the brook.

"O, Beautiful Willow Tree," said the little bird, "will you let me live in your warm branches until the springtime comes?"

"No, indeed," said the willow tree. "I never speak to strangers. Go away."

The poor little bird did not know where to go. He hopped and fluttered along with his broken wing. Presently the spruce tree saw him and said, "Where are you going, little bird?"

"I do not know," said the bird. "The other trees will not let me live with them. My wing is broken and I cannot fly."

"You may live on one of my branches," said the spruce. "Here is the warmest one of all."

"But may I stay all winter?"

"Yes," said the spruce. "I shall like having you."

The pine tree stood beside the spruce. When he saw the little bird hopping and fluttering with his broken wing, he said, "My branches are not very warm, but I can keep the wind off because I am big and strong."

So the little bird fluttered up into the warm branch of the spruce. The pine tree kept the wind off his house. Then the juniper tree saw what was going on. She said that she would give the little bird his dinner from her branches all winter. Juniper berries are very good for little birds.

The little bird was very comfortable in his warm nest sheltered from the wind with juniper berries to eat.

The trees at the edge of the forest remarked upon it to each other:

"I wouldn't take care of a strange bird," said the birch.

"I wouldn't risk my acorns," said the oak.

"I would not speak to strangers," said the willow. And the three trees stood up very tall and proud.

That night, the North Wind came to the woods to play. He puffed at the leaves with his icy breath. Every leaf he touched fell to the ground. He wanted to touch every leaf in the forest. He loved to see the trees bare.

"May I touch every leaf?" he said to his father, the Frost King.

"No," said the Frost King, "The trees which were kind to the bird with the broken wing may keep their leaves."

So North Wind had to leave them alone. The spruce, the pine, and the juniper tree kept their leaves throughout the winter. And they have done so ever since.

1. Why did the birds fly south?

    A. to find food
    B. to wait for spring
    C. to look for nests

2. What is the bird's problem?

    A. His wing is hurt.
    B. His friends have left.
    C. His nest is broken.

3. What tree does the bird go to first?

    A. the big oak
    B. the silver birch
    C. the beautiful willow

4. The willow tree let the bird stay because she

    A. always loses her leaves.
    B. doesn't think it will be warm enough.
    C. never talks to strangers.

5. How does the Juniper tree help the bird?

   A. She gives him berries.
   B. She keeps him warm.
   C. She blocks the wind.

6. What does this story teach about kindness? Use details from the story in your answer.

SAVING THE BIRDS

One day in spring, four men were riding on horseback along a country road. These men were lawyers. They were going to the next town to attend court.

It had rained. The ground was very soft. Water was dripping from the trees. The grass was <u>wet</u>.

The four lawyers rode along, one behind another. The pathway was narrow. The mud on each side of it was deep. They rode slowly. They talked and laughed and were very jolly.

As they were passing through a grove of small trees, they heard a great fluttering over their heads and a feeble chirping in the grass by the roadside.

"Stith! stith! stith!" came from the leafy branches above them.

"Cheep! cheep! cheep!" came from the wet grass.

"What is the matter here?" asked the first lawyer, whose name was Speed.

"Oh, it's only some old robins!" said the second lawyer, whose name was Hardin. "The storm has blown two of the little ones out of the nest. They are too young to fly, and the mother bird is making a great <u>fuss</u> about it."

"What a pity! They'll die down there in the grass," said the third lawyer, whose name I forget.

"Oh, well! They're nothing but birds," said Mr. Hardin. "Why should we bother?"

"Yes, why should we?" said Mr. Speed.

As they passed, the three men looked down and saw the little birds fluttering in the cold, wet grass. They saw the mother robin flying about and crying to her mate.

Then they rode on, talking and laughing as before. In a few minutes, they had forgotten about the birds.

The fourth lawyer, whose name was Abraham Lincoln, stopped. He got down from his horse and very gently took the little ones up in his big warm hands.

They did not seem frightened, but chirped softly, as if they knew they were safe.

"Never mind, my little fellows," said Mr. Lincoln "I will put you in your own cozy little bed."

Then he looked up to find the nest from which they had fallen. It was high, much higher than he could reach.

But Mr. Lincoln could climb. He had climbed many trees when he was a boy. He put the birds softly, one by one, into their warm little home. Two other baby birds, who had not fallen out, were there. All cuddled down together and were very happy.

Soon, the three lawyers who had ridden ahead stopped at a spring to give their horses water.

"Where is Lincoln?" asked one.

All were surprised to find that he was not with them.

"Do you remember those birds?" said Mr. Speed. "Very likely he has stopped to take care of them."

In a few minutes, Mr. Lincoln joined them. His shoes were covered with mud. He had torn his coat on the thorny tree.

"Hello, Abraham!" said Mr. Hardin. "<u>Where</u> have you been?"

"I stopped a minute to give those birds to their mother," he answered.

"Well, we always thought you were a hero," said Mr. Speed. "Now we know it."

Then all three of them laughed heartily. They thought it so foolish that a strong man should take so much trouble just for some worthless young birds.

"Gentlemen," said Mr. Lincoln, "I could not have slept tonight if I had left those helpless little robins to perish in the wet grass."

Abraham Lincoln afterwards became very famous as a lawyer and statesman. He was elected president of the United States. Next to George Washington, he was perhaps the greatest American.

1. What word sounds like the word <u>wet</u>?

    A. set
    B. with
    C. sad

2. This story is mostly about

    A. losing hope.
    B. helping birds.
    C. being happy.

3. In this story, the word <u>fuss</u> means

    A. mess.
    B. excite.
    C. bright.

4. Which word best describes Mr. Hardin?

    A. untidy
    B. lonely
    C. unkind

5. Mr. Lincoln helped the birds because he

   A. did not want them to be hurt.
   B. wanted his friend to see them.
   C. did not think they could fly.

6. Mr. Lincoln could climb well because he

   A. had strong legs.
   B. had climbed as a boy.
   C. climbed often as a man.

Read this sentence from the story.

> "Where have you been?"

7. Which word sounds the same as where?

   A. share
   B. wear
   C. were

8. Would you have helped the birds? Why or why not?

SPEAKING A PIECE

Two children, brother and sister, were on their way to school. Both were very small. The boy was only four years old. The girl was not yet six years old.

"Come, Edward, we must hurry," said the sister. "We must not be late." With one hand, the little boy clung to his sister's arm, and with the other he held his primer.

This primer was his only book and he loved it. It had a bright blue cover. He was careful not to soil it. In it were some odd little pictures. He never grew tired of looking at them.

Edward could spell nearly all the words in his primer and he could read quite well.

The school was more than a mile from their home. The children trotted along as fast as their short legs could carry them.

At a place where two roads crossed, they saw a tall gentleman coming to meet them. He was dressed in black and had a very pleasant face.

"Oh, Edward, there is Mr. Harris!" whispered the little girl. "Don't forget your manners."

They were glad to see Mr. Harris, for he was the minister. They stopped by the side of the road and made their manners. Edward bowed very gracefully and his sister curtsied.

"Good morning, children!" said the minister. He shook hands with each of them.

"I have something here for little Edward," he said. Then he took from his pocket a sheet of paper on which some verses were written.

"See! It is a little speech that I have written for him. The teacher will soon ask him to speak a piece at school. I am sure that he can learn this easily and speak it well."

Edward took the paper and thanked the kind minister.

"Mother will help him learn it," said his sister.

"Yes, I will try to learn it," said Edward.

"Do so, my child," said the minister; "and I hope that when you grow up you will become a wise man and a great orator."

Then the two children hurried on to school.

The speech was not hard to learn and Edward soon knew every word of it. When the time came for him to speak, his mother and the minister were both there to hear him.

He spoke so well that everybody was pleased. He pronounced every word plainly, as though he were talking to his schoolmates.

Here is Edward's speech:

> I'll tell a tale how Farmer John
> A little roan colt bred, sir,
> Which every night and every morn
> He watered and he fed, sir.
>
> Said Neighbor Joe to Farmer John,
> "You surely are a dolt, sir,
> To spend such time and care upon
> A little useless colt, sir."
>
> Said Farmer John to Neighbor Joe,
> "I bring my little roan up
> Not for the good he now can do,
> But will do when he's grown up."
>
> The moral you can plainly see,
> To keep the tale from spoiling,
> The little colt you think is me—
> I know it by your smiling.
>
> And now, my friends, please to excuse
> My lisping and my stammers;
> I, for this once, have done my best,
> And so—I'll make my manners.

That little boy's name was Edward Everett. He grew up to become a famous man and one of our greatest public speakers.

It had a bright blue cover.

1. Which word has two word parts?

   A. bright
   B. blue
   C. cover

2. What word means the same as <u>odd</u>?

   A. strange
   B. happy
   C. fast

3. Who gave Edward a speech?

   A. Mother
   B. Mr. Harris
   C. his sister

4. What does Mr. Harris hope for Edward?

   A. that he will be rich
   B. that he will be happy
   C. that he will be wise

5. Which word best describes the speech?

   A. hard
   B. nice
   C. sad

6. Do you think Edward would have grown up to be a great speaker even if he never gave this speech? Why or why not?

RAGGYLUG

Once there was a little furry rabbit. He lived with his mother deep down in a nest under the long grass. His name was Raggylug. His mother's name was Molly Cottontail. Every morning, when Molly Cottontail went out to hunt for food, she said to Raggylug, "Now, Raggylug, lie still and make no noise. No matter what you hear, no matter what you see, don't you move. Remember you are only a baby rabbit and lie low." And Raggylug always said he would.

One day, after his mother had gone, he was lying very still in the nest, looking up through the feathery grass. By just cocking his eye, he could see what was going on up in the world. Once a big blue jay perched on a twig above him and scolded someone very loudly. He kept saying, "Thief! thief!" But Raggylug never moved his nose or his paws. He lay still.

Once a lady bird took a walk down a blade of grass over his head. She was so top-heavy that pretty soon she tumbled off and fell to the bottom. She had to begin all over again. But Raggylug never moved his nose or his paws. He lay still.

The sun was warm. It was very still. Suddenly, Raggylug heard a little sound far off. It sounded like "*Swish, swish,*" very soft and far away. He listened. It was a queer little sound, low down in the grass, "*rustle—rustle—rustle.*" Raggylug was interested, but he never moved his nose or his paws. He lay still. Then the sound came nearer, "*rustle—rustle—rustle.*" Then it grew fainter. Then it came nearer, in and out, nearer and nearer, like something coming. Whenever Raggylug heard anything coming, he always heard its feet stepping ever so softly. What could it be that came so smoothly—*rustle—rustle*—without any feet?

He forgot his mother's warning. He sat up on his hind paws. The sound stopped then. "Pooh," thought Raggylug, "I'm not a baby rabbit. I am three weeks old. I'll find out what this is."

He stuck his head over the top of the nest and looked—straight into the wicked eyes of a great big snake. "Mammy, Mammy!" screamed Raggylug. "Oh, Mammy, Mam—" But he couldn't scream anymore. The big snake had his ear in his mouth and was winding about the soft little body, squeezing Raggylug's life out. He tried to call "Mammy!" again, but he could not breathe.

Ah, but Mammy had heard the first cry. Straight over the fields she flew, leaping the stones and hummocks, fast as the wind to save her baby. She wasn't a timid little cottontail rabbit then. She was a mother whose child was in danger. When she found Raggylug and the big snake, she took one look. Then hop! hop! she went over the snake's back. As she jumped, she struck at the snake with her strong hind claws so that they tore his skin. He hissed with rage, but he did not let go.

Hop! hop! she went again. This time she hurt the snake so that he twisted and turned, but he held on to Raggylug. Once more the mother rabbit hopped. Once more she struck and tore the snake's back with her sharp claws. *Zzz!* How she hurt! The snake dropped Raggy to strike at her. Raggy rolled on to his feet and ran.

"Run, Raggylug, run!" said his mother, keeping the snake busy with her jumps. You should have seen Raggylug ran! Just as soon as he was out of the way, his mother came, too. She showed him where to go. When she ran, there was a little white patch that showed under her tail. That was for Raggy to follow. He followed it now.

Far, far away she led him, through the long grass to a place where the big snake could not find him. There she made a new nest. And this time, when she told Raggylug to lie low, you'd better believe he minded!

1. Which word has the same ending sound as the word FURRY?

   A. happy
   B. berry
   C. funny

2. Molly Cottontail tells Raggylug to lie still so

   A. he can see other animals.
   B. other animals won't bother him.
   C. other animals won't hear him.

3. What causes Raggylug to move?

   A. a blue bird
   B. a strange sound
   C. a blade of grass

4. What made the sound?

   A. his mother
   B. a bird
   C. a snake

5. In this story, the word <u>danger</u> means

   A. trouble.
   B. strength.
   C. hopes.

6. Why didn't Raggylug move again?

   A. He didn't want to meet another snake.
   B. He didn't want to make another nest.
   C. He didn't want him mother in trouble.

Made in the USA
Middletown, DE
02 May 2024